Contemporary
CROSS-COUNTRY SKIING

Contemporary

CROSS-COUNTRY SKIING

Pat Thornton

cbi Contemporary Books, Inc.
Chicago

Library of Congress Cataloging in Publication Data

Thornton, Pat.
    Contemporary cross-country skiing.

    Includes index.
    1.   Cross-country skiing.   I. Title.
GV854.9.C7T525   1978   796.9'3   77-91175
ISBN 0-8092-7557-0
ISBN 0-8092-7646-1 pbk.

Published by Contemporary Books, Inc.
180 North Michigan Avenue, Chicago, Illinois 60601
Manufactured in the United States of America
Library of Congress Catalog Card Number: 77-91175
International Standard Book Number: 0-8092-7557-0 (cloth)
                                                      0-8092-7646-1 (paper)

Published simultaneously in Canada by
Beaverbooks
953 Dillingham Road
Pickering, Ontario L1W 1Z7
Canada

Dedicated to

All of those people who thought they couldn't ski because they had two left feet. May they now get off on the right foot and discover the wonders of a winter of cross-country skiing.

Contents

Contemporary
CROSS-COUNTRY SKIING

1

In the beginning

My first time on cross-country skis was a near disaster. Everything was wrong. Well, at least two major factors were wrong.

Wrong attitude

First, my attitude was not the best. I lived in Sun Valley, Idaho, one of the Alpine ski capitals of the world, and looked with almost disdain at this so-called sport that had little old ladies shuffling across the golf course. None of that stuff for me. I was too intent on learning the more daring, exciting, and, looking back, almost suicidal downhill skiing. Thus, I was less than enthusiastic about my magazine assignment on cross-country skiing.

Wrong outfit

The second thing that was wrong was my outfit. It was

the winter that *Vogue* magazine highlighted and Saks Fifth Avenue pushed knickers as *the* costume of the season. So, in my immaturity, I was slightly uplifted to think at least I could be fashionably dressed yet properly outfitted in Nordic ski style. However, once away from the picturesque glowing fireplace and out in the snow I realized those fashionable, nifty, double-knit knickers were not designed to stop the wind and keep out the cold of a January day in Idaho.

Otherwise, I was totally prepared for the cold—stocking cap that pulled down to the eyebrows, muffler that pulled up almost to the eyebrows, two sweaters, a cotton-knit turtleneck, a down-filled parka, three pairs of kneesocks, and a pair of giant furry mittens covering a pair of hand-knit woolen mittens. Any resemblance between me and Snohomish lies only in your imagination. I looked more like a frozen gorilla. Every joint except my knees (which were exposed to the elements through fashionable, nifty, double-knit knickers) was too well-padded to bend.

That was both good and bad. Good that the knee was free to flex and bend, because a soft knee is of prime importance in cross-country skiing. Bad that the other areas could not bend, because cross-country skiing is a loose, easy, fluid motion that encompasses the entire body. But the layers could be peeled off, and most of them did come off before my first lesson ended.

My instructor

The first lesson was a near disaster. What saved it was my instructor, a man uniquely qualified to teach cross-country skiing. He was born in Scandinavia and, typical of people of that area, learned to ski about the same time he learned to walk. In fact, during the long, snowy winters, cross-country skis were his only mode of transportation to school. Later he joined the ranks of competitors and became an international champion. Eventually, he took the natural

step into coaching and, like many of his countrymen, ultimately decided to share his knowledge with just plain folks.

The school was barely a month old that fateful day.
Near the end of that first lesson, my instructor suggested
taking a short tour and told me to fall in behind and try to
stay in his tracks. As we moved, I couldn't take my eyes off
the fluid form in front of me. He had the grace of a gazelle,
the rhythm of a calm ocean, and the steady motion of a
pendulum. I suddenly realized I was concentrating so much
on him and how he was moving that I had let my natural
movements take over. I was actually imitating without, of
course, the grace and coordination, but nevertheless, covering the miles and enjoying it. We stopped for a rest and I was
struck by the silence. We were well away from the crowds
on the mountain and ours were the only tracks in the snow,
save those left by some four-footed passersby.

I came away from that first lesson a believer in cross-
country skiing. I had learned a lot. And one of the most
important things I had learned was to start out right; not to
forge ahead blindly without knowing the basics. As the
saying goes, "If you can walk, you can cross-country ski," so
you probably wouldn't get hurt by charging forth, but you
won't have much fun, either. Just as in everything else, there
is a right way and a wrong way to cross-country ski, and the
pleasure comes in doing it right.

Beyond the first lesson

Since that first lesson I have learned some other things
about cross-country skiing. I found out it can be just as
daring, exciting, and satisfying, but not nearly as suicidal as
downhill skiing. As I became more proficient in both sports, I
happily divided my time between them. Some days I rode the
lifts to the top of the mountain and Alpined down; on other
days, I spent only 10 or 15 minutes scooting around the yard
or across the golf course. It was a good combination.

I also learned that downhill and cross-country skiing are very compatible. One helps the other. Many of the movements and turns are the same. The similarity is not too surprising when you stop to think about it. Both were developed in the Scandinavian countries. However, downhill skiing was adopted by the peoples of the Alps and became known as Alpine skiing, while cross-country skiing is still identified as Nordic.

History of skiing

Even that is ahead of the story because man has used skis as a mode of transportation for about 4,000 years. It's hard to believe, but archaeological digs above Sweden's Arctic Circle produced primitive skis that have been carbon-dated to 2000 B.C. Also, prehistoric cave drawings above the Arctic Circle indicate humans may have used the long bones of animals as skis. And still other evidence gives some indication that hunters wore one long ski for support and a short ski covered with fur to push themselves across the snow.

It wasn't until the middle of the nineteenth century that cross-country skis broke away from purely functional usage to become recreational tools. The first recorded cross-country ski race was in northern Norway in 1843; and the Holmenkollen jumping and skiing event, one of the biggest winter happenings in Europe, premiered in 1892 on the outskirts of Oslo.

Cross-country skis are not new in the United States either. They were introduced before the Civil War by Scandinavian immigrants who carried them to every part of the country. You've heard the U.S. Post Office's saying that neither rain nor sleet nor snow will stop the mail. Well, cross-country skis were an aid in making sure the mail did go through. During the gold rush days Norwegian-born Jon Torsteinson was the only winter link between mining camps in Nevada and civilization in California. He became known as John "Snowshoe" Thompson and, for 20 years, carried mail over the Sierra Mountains from Placerville, California, to Carson City, Nevada, on skis he made himself. The trip took three days and it is said he never missed a trip because of illness.

Skis of today are a far cry from what "Snowshoe" Thompson wore, but the technique hasn't changed much. It is still a smooth, rhythmic, loose movement that can be mastered by people of all ages, sizes, and shapes, levels of coordination, temperament, and skills. That, in itself, may explain the increasing popularity of cross-country skiing.

I got hooked on it during one lesson and enthusiastically pursued the sport, even to the point of citizen racing. I was fortunate enough to have had the benefit of superb instruction my first time out, therefore this book is based on what I learned then and in subsequent years of skiing and racing. It is designed to help you avoid some of the pitfalls uneducated beginners often encounter. One word of caution, however: Cross-country skiing can be habit-forming.

Robert E. Lee

2
Equipment

There is no mystique about cross-country ski equipment. It is light in weight, usually costs less than Alpine equipment, and does not require a lot of frills. In fact, unless you are planning a mountain climbing excursion, the lighter and less equipment you pack along, the more comfortable and carefree you are going to be and the more you are going to enjoy yourself. The difference is the same as running ten miles wearing waffle stompers as opposed to nylon jogging shoes. Why pack around the extra weight if you don't need it?

The basic cross-country ski equipment required for a spin around the golf course or a trip through the park is boots, skis, bindings, and poles. That's it. Nothing else. Naturally, the better skier you become and the farther afield you go, the more equipment you will want and need. But the logical question at this point is: What do I buy? The answer is: Nothing, if you can avoid it.

The very best way to begin cross-country skiing is with rented equipment. This enables you to learn what best suits you for your particular kind of skiing and whether or not you enjoy the sport enough to buy your own equipment. Nordic ski equipment runs the gamut from light, virtually level touring to heavy, up-and-down mountainside skiing to competition. So, if at all possible, get the basics down without a lot of investment, then buy whatever paraphernalia meets your skiing requirements.

Remember, however, that mountaineering and competition are the two extremes of Nordic skiing, and the equipment designed for them is neither good nor practical for general touring. Gear used in mountaineering is heavy and rigid, while that used for competition is light and fragile. So I'll concentrate on the basic touring outfits and, because gear changes each season, I'll discuss generalities rather than specifics. Most cross-country ski shopkeepers are very well-versed in what is new and what is good on the current market, so don't be afraid to ask them. No question is silly or dumb when you want an answer. Here, then, are some basics:

Boots

Boots are the key to good skiing. They are the most important equipment you will use, so select carefully and wisely. If you are going to buy boots, buy the best ones available. You can cut costs somewhere else.

Boots, as with skis, are designed to meet the requirements of use, so decide what kind of skiing you want to do, then buy the boots accordingly. In general, you will find Nordic boots to be much lighter in weight and more flexible than Alpine boots. And you're apt to find them as comfortable as well-broken-in jogging shoes.

When being fitted for boots, wear the socks you will be wearing while skiing because fit is very important. Boots should be snug but not tight in width and there should be plenty of toe room. Boots that are too big or too small will cause blisters; and boots that are too small will definitely inhibit circulation and literally give you cold feet. Generally speaking, if you can put a finger behind the heel with your toes touching the front of an unlaced boot, the fit is good.

Lace up the boots and stand up. With your weight on the left foot, raise the heel of the right foot, then transfer your weight to the ball of the right foot. The front of the right boot should flex easily and form a crease across the toe (Figure 2.1). If you can feel the crease rubbing, try a larger size. You also can test for size by standing on an incline facing downhill. If your foot slides forward away from the heel, try a smaller size. Another test is to lace up the boots and then try to work your heel up and down inside the boot while holding the outside. If you can move the heel, try a smaller size.

In addition to fitting properly, the boots should have a side-to-side rigidity. Test this by twisting the boot as you would a rag. If it twists easily, it is too flexible and you should try a different pair. Look for one that has a metal strip along the sole to maintain rigidity.

Boots come in a variety of materials—leather and rubber, plastic and other man-made fibers. All have advantages, but the most important consideration is that the upper part of the boots can breathe. Rubber and plastic are fine for

crease

Figure 2.1. Testing the fit of the boot. If it rubs the top of the foot at the crease, it is too small.

keeping the wet snow out, but they also keep the wet perspiration in, which results in cold feet. Leather, of course, breathes, but it also requires proper care: Shake the snow off, stuff the boots with crumpled newspapers, and allow them to dry in a warm place away from direct heat. When thoroughly dry, replace the newspaper with a shoe tree or put the boots on a ski-boot press. A good leather conditioner or polish and a good waterproofer should be applied now and again. But never plug up the pores with grease or self-shining coatings.

Remember, a bargain in boots is not necessarily a bargain. Shop wisely.

Skis

What makes cross-country skis different from downhill skis is the construction of the bottom of the skis. Nordic skis have something that "grips" the snow so the skier can get a

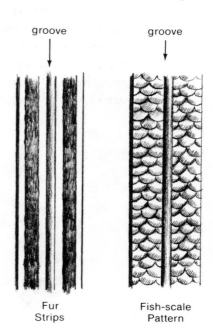

Figure 2.2.   Two of several types of nonwax bottoms available on cross-country skis.

good forward-motion push. The "gripper" can be wax or strips of fur or mohair, or it can be fish-scale patterns, step-patterns, or replaceable fur strips (Figure 2.2).

Here's how the gripper works: You've probably noticed that skis are bowed in the middle. That's called *camber* and it allows the ski bottoms to rise off the surface of the snow when the skier takes body weight off the ski. When the skier transfers the body weight back to that ski, the gripper reaches down and sticks to or grabs the snow so the skier doesn't go backwards. The action also forms a platform from which the skier can push off.

Waxing or not waxing

Ask a group of cross-country skiers which bottoms they prefer, and most likely you'll hear an argument about the virtues of wax versus nonwax bases. What it all boils down to is a matter of personal preference. Ask yourself the following questions: How much of a purist are you? How much time do you have to devote to preparing your skis?

As with virtually everything in this day and age, modern technology has invaded the cross-country ski industry— to the chagrin of the purists but to the delight of the occasional recreational skier. The biggest change in skis in the past several years is in the materials from which the skis themselves are made. Originally all Nordic skis were wood and required a sealing pine tar base and waxes. Today, all-wood skis are tough to find, and if you already own a matched pair, you may wish to cross them above the fireplace as a collector's item. Modern skis are of man-made materials or, occasionally, a combination of wood and man-made fibers. And you have a choice of waxing or not waxing.

In making that choice, several factors must be considered. Waxing takes time, requires a basic understanding of snow conditions, and knowledge of the type of wax required for the day's excursion. Once you get going, waxed skis are better running and faster because the bottoms are smooth.

For purely recreational skiing, I prefer the nonwax base because I can clamp on my skis and be on my way in just a matter of minutes. Besides, I don't run the risk of putting on the wrong color of wax and having an uncomfortable day because the snow is balling on the bottom of my skis or my skis are not gripping. (Incidentally, I always carry along a stick of everyday, household paraffin in case changing temperatures and snow conditions cause icing on my nonwax skis. Just rub it on the bottom, being careful not to get the paraffin on the fur or pattern or in the long groove.)

On the other hand, my racing skis are wax base because I'm more interested in speed. The drag of the gripper may be the difference in placing or not. Besides, a race is usually skied in a much shorter time frame so snow conditions are not as likely to change as dramatically as during a day tour.

These are strictly my opinions. Some of my friends feel otherwise. They are challenged by waxing and wouldn't be caught skiing on nonwax bases. Get skis that you will be comfortable with and don't let anyone talk you into one kind or another; the choice is strictly up to you. If you are in doubt, try to rent both kinds and judge for yourself.

How to wax

If you lean toward wax, jump right in and start learning. Wax is a paste that, when applied correctly, grips the snow and allows the ski to glide as pressure is applied and released. In other words, when you apply pressure by stepping on the ski, the wax sticks to the snow; when you take your weight off, the wax releases the grip and the ski glides.

The most important part of waxing is applying the correct wax. The structure of both snow and wax is crystalline, but the snow changes its structure when variations occur in temperature, pressure, and light. That is why freshly fallen snow is different from old snow, snow in the sun is different from snow in the shade, and snow at higher altitudes is different from snow in lower altitudes. Furthermore, snow can be both viscous, or sticky, as well as elastic.

Wax is stable, which is why changing snow conditions call for different waxes. The correct wax is the one that allows the right amount of glide combined with the right kick. Because both wax and snow are crystalline, the action comes through the crystalline binding of the wax with the snow. If the two interlock too much, the wax is too soft and sticks to the snow. If the two do not interlock enough, there is no grip at all. So the right choice is very important.

When in doubt, always use a colder wax. Remember that soft or warm wax can be applied on top of hard or cold wax, but hard wax cannot be applied on top of soft (Figure 2.3). The best way to learn about waxes is to stick to one brand until you know its strong points and its weak ones. Experiment with colors, but don't mix brands because no two colors are alike.

Also, when applying wax, remember that the thicker the layer of wax, the better the grip; but the thicker the layer of wax, the less the glide.

Figure 2.3. When too soft a wax is used, snow will adhere to the skis, inhibiting any movement—forward or back. When in doubt, always use the harder wax.

Ski shapes and sizes

A touring ski is usually slightly wider at the tips and tails than it is in the middle and usually narrower and longer than an Alpine ski. Although the length of a Nordic ski is not as important, it should be taken into consideration. If you are old enough to remember downhill skiing of 40 years ago, you already know how to judge the length of your cross-country skis: Stand erect on the floor and raise one arm straight overhead. With the tail of the ski resting on the floor next to your feet, the tip should hit midpalm of your upraised hand (Figure 2.4).

Skis come in 5 centimeter increments, so if your midpalm is somewhere between sizes, consider the following: A shorter ski is easier to control; longer skis facilitate a longer glide. A longer ski offers additional carrying surface for a heavier skier; a lighter person may prefer a shorter ski.

Bindings

Boots are attached to skis through bindings that are

Figure 2.4. Measure the ski length. It should reach midpalm when your hand is straight overhead.

Figure 2.5. Most Nordic boots have holes in the top sole to accomodate pin, mousetrap, or pole-operated bindings.

Figure 2.6. Top view of pin bindings. (a) The clamp holding the wire locked down. (b) The wire that fits down on the top of the boot sole, holding it in place. (c) Three pins that fit into the holes of the boot sole.

light in weight and allow the heel to move up and down freely. The most popular for touring are known as mouse-trap, pin, or pole-operated bindings. They are one-and-the-same and come in a one-size-fits-all "norm fit," which means the soles of cross-country boots—be they ladies' size 5 or men's size 12—are the same and fit the same sized bindings. This, or course, is of great advantage in ski swapping or ski sharing.

The three holes in the toe-end of the boot sole (Figure 2.5) fit into the three pins on the base of the bindings (Figure 2.6); the mousetrap-like wire clamps down on top of the boot sole and one never has to bend over because it can all be done by the tip of the pole.

Poles

The equipment that probably gets rougher treatment than any other is the poles. They help you push uphill, speed you on your way across the flat, drag to slow your downhill speed, and lift you out of the snow after you have probably sat on them. It is no wonder, then, that experts recommend getting a high-quality aluminum pole for touring. They caution against buying cheap or inexpensive aluminum poles, however, because they are simply not good buys. Tonkin or bamboo poles should be avoided, too, because they tend to break.

Good quality aluminum poles combine lightness and liveliness with strength and durability. They may cost a little more initially, but are a good value in the long run.

The tip of the pole is supposed to be bent (that's not a defect) so it can be extracted from the snow more easily. There should be a basket or metal ring just above the tip,

Figure 2.8. Measure the length of the pole by stretching your arm straight out, parallel to the floor. Your forearm should rest comfortably on it.

Figure 2.7. Nordic ski poles have an (a) adjustable wrist strap, (b) basket to prevent the pole from sinking too far into the snow, and (c) a bent tip for easy extraction from the snow.

which keeps the pole from sinking too far into the snow. And there should be an adjustable loop strap firmly attached to the handle (Figure 2.7).

The length of the pole is an important factor in the skier's performance. If the pole is too long it will hinder style and if it is too short the skier will be too bent over. A rule of thumb in selecting poles is to figure a maximum length as 12 inches less than the skier's height. But the easiest way to test fit is to have the pole fit snugly under your armpit. Stand on the floor with the pole upright to and slightly away from the body. Raise your arm straight out, parallel to the ground and rest your forearm on top of the pole (Figure 2.8). If you are between sizes, take the longer pole. And if everything seems too long at the store, remember when you are skiing, the pole sinks into the snow.

Clothing

"What do I wear?" The answer is simple: Whatever you want or whatever you've got. However, you will want to be clad in layers of loose-fitting clothing. Don't go out and buy a whole wardrobe of new Nordic clothes until you have read this book the whole way through and have cross-country skied at least twice. As incredible as it may sound, there is always that remote possibility you won't like this sport. So leave your clothing allowance in the piggy bank for the time being and wear whatever you already have while you are skiing on rented equipment.

Now I'm going to make that inevitable exception: If you can't rent gaiters, buy 'em. They are relatively inexpensive and, to my way of thinking, a pair of gaiters is one of the best investments in cross-country ski equipment. If you are unfamiliar with them, gaiters are water-repellent cloth that snugly cover the boot top, ankle, instep, and at least part of the lower leg. In appearance, they resemble spats of olden days. What they do is keep snow from getting down inside the boot and, thus, keep your feet dry.

Select clothing that offers freedom of movement, warmth, and comfort. Avoid man-made fabrics that don't breathe. Although blue jeans are fine to wear in the beginning, you will want to avoid them later because they soak up moisture. Tight stretch-pants should be avoided, too, because they inhibit movement.

A beginner Alpine skier spends half of his time in the snow and, therefore, finds water-repellent clothing a necessity. To fall in Nordic skiing is rare, but you'll want water-repellent outer garments anyway. You could always get caught in a snowstorm. Remember that water-repellent is better than waterproof—any material that is truly waterproof can't breathe, and you need that ventilation.

Nordic experts recommend several layers of loose-fitting clothing that can be peeled off as desired. The advice is good. Remember, thick is not necessarily warm, and perspiration and cold are your worst enemies, so dressing in layers is of highest importance. As you get warm or cool, you can subtract or add layers to maintain a comfort level.

I usually wear two pairs of socks—lightweight cotton inside to absorb perspiration and knee-high woolen stockings outside. If it's a wet day or if you are going on a longer tour, it is always nice to have a spare pair along.

Knickers, of course, are the preferred pants because they permit the necessary flexibility of the knee. Light knickers of wool, corduroy, or even poplin are ideal. Some skiers insist upon wearing long-johns, but unless I'm going to take an exceptionally long tour in extremely cold weather, I don't bother.

The upper part of your body will be comfortable if it is covered by layers. Many serious skiers prefer net underwear because it creates an insulating layer of air between skin and clothing. A cotton T-shirt also works well against the skin. Add a light turtleneck, then a woolen shirt, and then a windshell or parka.

Extremities are important. Close, but not tight-fitting,

leather gloves are good for warmer days, but mittens are what you will want on cold days. Look for cross–country mittens with both a liner and a shell that can be worn together or separately. The best have liners of silk or light-weight wool with leather shells. They are very flexible and toasty warm.

Do wear a hat. A tremendous amount of body heat floats right out the top of your head, so don't take a chance on catching cold. And when you're picking it out, be sure the hat can be pulled down over your ears.

3
How to start

You've already heard, "If you can walk, you can cross-country ski." It's true. Cross-country skiing is one of the most natural sports in which you can participate, and the only one I know of, besides plain walking, that does not require extraordinary conditioning to start. The pace is yours—as fast or as slow as you want to go, stopping whenever you want to catch your breath or to look around.

Skiing as a conditioner

Skiing, itself, is a conditioner. It's an exercise that uses all parts of the body—legs, arms, torso, heart, lungs—and helps develop muscle tone, but not muscle bulge. Have you ever seen a serious cross-country skier who was fat? Or one that looked like a Russian weight lifter? You're not likely to, either. Cross-country skiing is a sport of the svelte. It's a great calorie burner, too.

Covert Bailey, one of the country's leading authorities

on nutrition and physical fitness, calls cross-country skiing the "king of the aerobic exercises." He says it offers all of the benefits of running without any of the bad effects.

Of course, while skiing is a conditioner, the better physical condition you are in to begin with, the more comfortable you will be and the more you will enjoy cross-country skiing. Anything that improves your physical fitness is a perfect exercise.

Getting in shape

There are many things you can do, and now is the best time to start. Get up out of that chair, rise up on your tiptoes, and reach your arms up toward the ceiling. Stretch. Relax. Stretch. Relax. That little stretching exercise is typical of what you can do in the confines of an apartment or an office, and the possibilities are virtually endless.

Isometrics—pitting one set of muscles against another—can be done unobtrusively at almost any time. Example: Make a fist with your right hand and press it into the palm of your left; push one against the other. At the same time, take a deep breath and hold it a full count of three; exhale deeply.

If you are already a jogger, you're miles ahead. If you are not, get started. If you have been especially sedentary, start slowly with just a short, easy walk and gradually build up to brisk strides. If you live in the city and ride the bus, get off a stop or two early. If you work in an office building, get off the elevator a floor or two short in both directions. If you live in a small town, walk to the grocery instead of driving.

Jumping rope is one of the better forms of exercise for helping build not only the legs and arms, but the cardiovascular system as well. And it can be done in the confines of your own home. Be sure to wear shoes when you jump rope and, if you can, jump to music; that is much more pleasant.

For variation, try bicycling, swimming, tennis, or racquetball. These are all good ways to better condition yourself, not only for cross-country skiing, but for your general health and well-being, too. If you are near a YMCA, ask if a fitness program is offered. Many Y's have excellent, carefully planned and well-monitored programs for developing cardiovascular fitness, muscle tone, and endurance.

Whatever fitness program you undertake, be sure it is right for you and your physical condition at the moment. Do not overdo. Don't force yourself to the point of hating the exercise; if it is drudgery you won't keep it up. Get into a program you can live with and stick to it. Working out three days with a day off in between each week is a good way to develop and maintain a good physical level. Be sure to warm

Figure 3.1. Try this exercise to strengthen your legs and to get used to bending your knees. You're in shape if you can hold the position four minutes.

up properly before vigorous exercise and, just as important, warm down afterwards.

Specifics for skiing

Now for some specifics that will help your skiing. Balance is important to cross-country skiing, so work at improving it. For example, try to walk along a railroad track or a railing or a log for some distance. Can you balance a yardstick upright in the palm of your hand? On your chin?

You will need to strengthen your legs and get into the habit of bending your knees. This exercise is helpful: With your back leaning against the wall, pretend you are sitting in a chair, with your lower legs vertical to the floor and your thighs parallel to it. Hold that position. If you're lucky, you can "sit" like that for about 15 seconds. When you are in

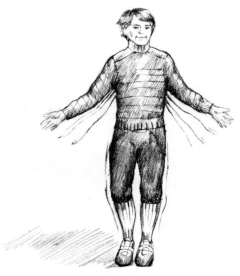

Figure 3.2a. Bounce up and down, bending your knees and allowing your arms to swing together.

Figure 3.2b. Bounce up and down, bending your knees; swing one arm forward, the other arm back in rhythm with your bounce.

shape, you will probably be able to hold it for four minutes (Figure 3.1).

Here's another exercise that will help you with your natural rhythm. Stand with your weight evenly divided on the balls of both feet. Hang loose and bounce up and down by bending your knees. What's happening to your arms? They are swinging back and forth together in a natural motion. Now, as you continue to bounce, swing first your right arm forward, then your left, in this same natural rhythm with the up and down bounce of your knees (Figure 3.2 a & b). This exercise is the most important thing you've done so far. It is the introduction to the natural rhythm of cross-country skiing.

Canadian Government Office of Tourism

4

The first time on cross-country skis

If you have never been on skis before, you are about to encounter a very strange sensation—the feeling your feet suddenly have grown to outlandish proportions. Until you become familiar with the idea of having skis as extensions of your own feet, you will probably find that they can all too easily become crossed in front—and in back, too. And you will discover that the top ski must move before the bottom one can.

One of the beauties of cross-country skiing is that you can do it almost anywhere there are a few inches of snow on a soft base. Stay away, of course, from gravel or concrete or other rough surfaces that don't have a sufficient snow covering to protect the bottoms of your skis. You do not need a mountain with lifts to enjoy this sport; your backyard, a golf course, or any other fairly level, relatively treeless spot is a perfect place to start.

Putting the skis on

Look at the bindings on your skis. One will be marked with an "R" or "Right" and the other will be marked "L" or "Left." Regardless of what it looks like, there is a difference in the bindings, so lay them down in the snow on the correct sides.

Now, look for the three little bumps or "pins" on the bindings. You already know they fit into the three holes on the toe sole of your boot, which you have already cleared of snow. Slip your toe over the pins until they catch. That wire or clamp on top of the bindings is where the bindings get one of their names—mousetrap. They work like an old-fashioned mousetrap: The wire fits down on top of the sole, holding the boot securely, and snaps into the catch in front (Figure 4.1). That's it, you've got one ski on. Do the other. Now you are ready to begin learning to cross-country ski.

Using the poles

Pick up your poles and hold them in any fashion that will help you maintain your balance. (There is a right and a wrong way to hold your poles. However, since you have so much to concentrate on in the beginning, you will begin by

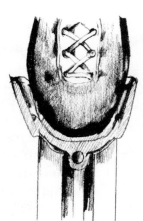

Figure 4.1. Mousetrap bindings clamp down over the top of the sole, holding the boot in place.

Figure 4.2. Using the poles at the side for balance, bend one knee and lift the leg. The ski tip is in the air, but the tail is still on the ground.

using your poles only for balance.) Plant one pole upright in the snow on either side; pick up one foot. Just bend your knee and lift the foot off the ground. What is happening, besides having to lean on the poles for balance? The ski tip is in the air, but the tail is still on the ground (Figure 4.2). Put your foot back down and look at the boot and the binding. Now lift just your heel. It's loose and comes up easily because only the toe of the boot is clamped in the binding. The heel can move freely up and down, exactly the same as it does when you are walking on the ball of your foot.

Congratulations! You have just experienced the first principle of cross-country skiing: You carry your weight on the balls of your feet, thus unencumbering your heels, allowing them to move freely up and down.

Moving the skis

Now, try this exercise: With your weight on your right foot, slide your left ski forward, causing your right knee to bend. Where is your right heel? It is in the air, well off the ski (Figure 4.3). Switch legs. With your weight on your left foot, slide your right ski slightly forward, causing your left

Figure 4.3. Slide one ski back and forth. As your knee bends, the heel lifts off the ski—a basic principle of Nordic skiing.

knee to flex and your heel to lift. Repeat this exercise several times until you feel comfortable and fairly secure on your skis.

If you can, slide the left ski forward enough that your right knee comes down to the right ski. Repeat with the right ski forward, left knee coming down (Figure 4.4). This, incidentally, is a wonderful warm-up exercise; many profes-

Figure 4.4 Slide one ski so far forward that the opposite knee almost touches the ski. This is good practice and a good warm-up exercise. Keep poles at the side for balance.

sionals do this exercise almost daily before setting off on their skis.

Now with your weight on your left foot, raise your right foot several inches off the snow. What is the ski's position? The tip is in the air and the tail is still on the ground. Can you make the ski level and parallel to the ground? Point your toes down; the ski tail comes up (Figure 4.5). See how easy it is to control the ski? Put the ski down and try the same thing with the other foot. Shift your weight to your right foot and raise your left. Point your toes and bring the ski level. Return to a standing position. Repeat at least once more on both sides or until you are comfortable and able to maintain your balance.

Pick up your right ski again, but this time, instead of putting it down beside the left, side-step several inches to the right, then put it down. Bring the left ski to it, being careful not to let the skis cross. Repeat. Now go the opposite direction. Repeat again only this time use little quick steps.

Side-step again, this time spreading the tails of your skis and forming a V with the tips. Pick up the right ski, move it

Figure 4.5. Point toes down to bring the ski parallel to the snow. Practice this to develop control of the skis.

Figure 4.6. Slide-step in a circle by forming a V with the tips of the skis.

several inches to the right, and put it down, tips together and tails apart. Bring the left ski to it (Figure 4.6). Repeat until you have gone a complete 360 degrees. Congratulations! You have just made your first turn on cross-country skis. Make another circle, this time going in the opposite direction.

Now make another circle, but this time form the V with the tails of your skis; repeat in the opposite direction (Figure 4.7).

These are all terrific exercises which enable you to become familiar and comfortable with your equipment. The easier and more natural you find it is to handle your skis, the more you will relax.

Moving forward

Now try to move forward. Pick out an object—a tree, rock, bush, fencepost—no more than 50 yards away and "walk" to it. Right, just take a simple walk on your skis, using all of those natural, subconscious movements you use when not encumbered by skis. Don't think about it, just do

Figure 4.7. Make another circle by side-stepping, but form the V with the tails of the skis.

it. The skis will come along naturally. Start with your weight on the left foot and slide the right foot forward a couple of feet, or slightly less than a normal stride. Keeping the skis on the ground, just slide them and allow the heel to come up naturally. Shift all of your body weight to the right leg and step on the ski (Figure 4.8). Slide your left foot forward, transfer your weight and step on it. Repeat and repeat until you have reached your goal.

See, there's really no trick to it. I keep telling you cross-country skiing is a very natural thing to do. I'll give you one

Figure 4.8. Take a short walk by just sliding one ski forward, then the other.

Right   Wrong

Figure 4.9.   Watch your body position. Try to stay square over your skis.

hint though: do not overreach with your forward foot. Beginners have a tendency to try to reach too far. Just use your normal walking stride. Your body position should be square over the skis and the knee should be soft. As a rule of thumb, you should be able to see the tip of your boot below your bent knee, but not your stockings (Figure 4.9). If you get behind your skis you will have a tendency to lose control.

Remember that side-step circle you made? Do it again, but only halfway around. Now ski back so you are facing the point from which you started. You should find this a little easier. One reason is that you are using the tracks you made on the way out, and it is always easier to ski in tracks than it is to ski in virgin snow.

Turn around and ski that track again, and this time really relax. Use the exercise in which you bounced up and down in your knees and let your arms swing in their natural

Figure 4.10.   Cross-country motion is a game of opposites—right leg, left arm forward, then left leg, right arm forward.

way. Start by standing still; begin bouncing in your knees, up and down, up and down. Get the rhythm and begin your forward motion. Your knees should be soft and your arms should be swinging with the opposite leg (Figure 4.10). Left foot, right arm forward; right foot, left arm forward. Bend your knees. Push a little with the balls of your feet. Your heels should be moving freely up and down on and off the skis.

Balance

One of the best ways to improve your skiing is to look where you are going. If you are watching your feet, you will never make it. Look at least one ski length ahead and you will notice an instant improvement. You will have much better balance, for one thing, and you will see something more interesting than your boots. Later on, as you become a better skier, you will do the natural thing—look at the scenery around you.

By now you should have the feel of it and, although the skis are narrow, you probably have reasonably good natural balance. To develop that balance even further, get rid of your poles. Stand them in the snow. With arms straight out to the side, do your knee bends—one ski forward, the

Figure 4.11. Without poles, arms stretched wide for balance, slide one ski forward so the opposite knee almost touches the ski.

35

opposite knee coming down to touch the ski (Figure 4.11). Standing, lift one ski, level it, return it to the snow; repeat with the opposite ski. Do a series of quick little side-steps to the right; repeat to the left. Make a circle around the tips of your skis in both directions. Make a circle around the tails in both directions. Ski the length of the track and back.

Try it again without poles. Go the length of the track, but this time, really exaggerate the bend in the knees and the swing of the arms. Once you have this rhythm down, you will have a good foundation for your ski touring, and you will never forget it.

If you've been practicing this exercise properly, you probably have gotten a little glide with each step. That is what you are ultimately looking for. That is what Nordic skiing is all about.

Still without poles, start out on a new track and make a large figure eight pattern. Now, go around the figure eight with an exaggerated swinging of the arms and a deep bend of the knees. As you go into a turn, push off with your outside foot (making a turn to the right, the outside foot would be the left one) and glide around the turn. Begin with your weight on the outside foot, step down, then push off; transfer your weight to the inside foot as you glide. The push is the same motion used to push off in ice skating.

The natural thing to do when you push off is to transfer your weight to the forward ski. That is also the correct thing to do because the total transfer of body weight is the essence of cross-country skiing. That's where the glide comes from.

Poles

Now that you know you don't need your poles for balance, it is time to pick them up again. This time, let's do it the right way.

The poles were designed as an aid to the skier to help get that extra push in going uphill, to get that extra speed in going across the flat, to slow the speed in going downhill, and to help lift yourself out of the snow in the event you have fallen.

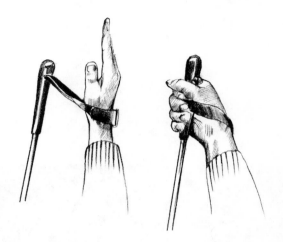

Figure 4.12. With thumb up, hand open, reach up through leather loop. Then close hand around strap and pole.

To take up your poles properly, remember one cardinal rule: Do not just grab onto them. That strap fastened to the top of the handle was made to go over your wrist to hold the pole when you let go of it and to keep your hand from slipping down the pole too far. The strap is adjustable, so open it wide enough that you can slip your hand through it, reaching from the bottom up. Open your hand wide, thumb up, with the palm toward the pole. Let the strap fall around your wrist. Close your hand around the strap and the pole (Figure 4.12). Check the length of the strap to be sure it holds the hand from slipping below the handle.

With poles in hand, repeat everything you did without poles, thinking of them merely as extensions of your hands.

Review

Reviewing what you have learned thus far: Your knees should be soft and flexible; your arms should swing forward and back with the opposite legs; your weight should transfer completely from one ski to the other. You should have a slightly forward lean and be square over your skis. Allow your heels to lift, just as they do when you walk.

This seems like a lot to remember, so the trick is to forget about it, stay loose, and do what comes naturally. Everything will fall into place.

5

Moving forward

How do you feel? I hope you feel reasonably comfortable and stable on your skis, and that you are relaxed and loose, with your knees bending with each stride. Or, do you look like a frozen gorilla—arms glued to the body, legs straight like sticks from ankle to thigh? If you are skiing like an Arctic version of King Kong, do not pass GO and do not collect $200. Go back and review the last chapter. However, if you are moving relaxed with good soft knees and your arms are swinging in their natural rhythm, read on.

Diagonal stride

It is a joy to watch a top-notch Nordic skier use diagonal stride to move gracefully across gentle rolling terrain in an almost slow motion rhythm. He seems to do it so effortlessly. If you do it right, with practice you will look like that too someday. So let us start right now.

Did you ever ride a scooter when you were a kid

Figure 5.1 The basic push-and-glide motion is similar to that used on riding a scooter or the push-off in ice skating.

(Figure 5.1)? Even if you didn't, try this exercise: Push your left ski slightly ahead. With most of your weight on your left foot, push yourself forward with the ball of your right foot. Coast and enjoy the ride. Keep your weight on the left side and push again with the ball of your right foot. Glide until you come to a stop.

Now think about what you just did. Your right knee had to be bent and the heel of your right foot was well off your ski. Your weight was on the forward ski. Try the same thing again on the opposite side. Stand with your right ski weighted and push off with the ball of your left foot. Glide. When you begin to slow down, push again with your left foot. Glide.

Repeat the exercise again, but with this variation: Push with the ball of your right foot and allow your weight to follow its natural forward motion to the left ski, which will be slightly ahead. Glide. With your weight on the left ski, slide the right one slightly forward, pushing with the ball of your left foot and allow your weight to follow its natural forward motion to the right ski. Glide. Shift your weight to the left, forward ski as you push off with the right. Glide. Left push, glide. Right push, glide. Just like ice skating, isn't it?

What were your arms doing as you were stepping from ski to ski? Were they moving naturally with your steps— right leg, left arm; left leg, right arm? Good!

Congratulations! You were doing the basic cross-country technique known as diagonal stride. Almost everything you learn about ski touring from here on out will have its roots in diagonal stride. It is the most basic and most important element that, when done properly, makes touring almost effortless.

The kick

In cross-country skiing, that force you get by pushing with the ball of one foot and, thus, propelling yourself forward is called the kick. Basically, it is a two-leg motion and must include a complete transfer of body weight from one ski to the other. Momentarily you are gliding on one ski, with the entire body weight centered on that ski.

Remember it this way: As you finish pushing off with the rear foot, the shift of weight to the forward, or opposite, ski would have already happened. At first, you will probably not go very far, but eventually, the shift in weight combined with a good stride will probably make the tail of the back, now-unweighted ski lift off the snow.

Experts argue whether the ski should be allowed to lift, or whether it should be kept in contact with the snow. Most say to keep it on the snow to start. Later you may want to allow the lift, which is both more efficient and grand looking when you are skiing on a good, hard track with skis that are either properly waxed or have a good commercially made nonwax base. So practice with your push-off kick and be very happy if (a) you go more than several inches, (b) both skis stay flat on the snow, and (c) you have developed good enough balance to glide along on one ski.

Figure 5.2. Quick Ski exercise will help develop a fast kicking motion. Use your arms to help "pump."

Quick ski

Lay your poles down here and do this exercise:

Bend your elbows and hold your arms at about a 90-degree angle. Now, move around the track with short, quick strides, helping yourself along like a sprinter who pumps his arms up and down (Figure 5.2). Your skis will have a tendency to come up as you take these quick steps; let them. You should be able to feel yourself developing a strong kick. As you improve, try to get the feeling that your hip is swinging forward with the knee, similar to a pendulum.

Still without poles, try the quick ski again, but allow yourself some glide along with it. Here's how: Combine the powerful kick with the forward thrust you are developing with a nice, relaxed glide. Take two or three quick ski steps, then glide. Be sure your knees are soft. Enjoy the ride (Figure 5.3). Just before the glide comes to a stop and your momentum is almost gone, do another kick. Repeat. Step, push, glide. Step, push, glide. Are your arms going with the opposite leg? Very good! You are doing the diagonal stride and well on your way.

Figure 5.3.   Do the Quick Ski again, but allow yourself some glide along with it.

Poling

The next step is to put your poles to use. You already have noticed the bend in your pole between the basket ring and the tip. It was made that way on purpose. With the tip bent as it is, combined with the angle at which the pole is set in the snow and subsequently brought out again, there is less resistance. What that means to you is that the pole won't get stuck in the snow, particularly when there is an icy crust. The bend, then, simply allows the pole to be freed more easily from the snow.

You already know how to take up your poles. It is important to hold them loosely. Don't hang on to them for dear life—you'll get cramps in your fingers, cut off circula-

Note the proper angle.

Figure 5.4.   In using your poles, your hand will be slightly forward of the ring.

tion, and maybe stab a low-flying bird. So hold the poles lightly, preferably with just the thumb and forefinger. To help familiarize yourself with the poles, keeping them parallel to the ground and standing still, bounce up and down in your knees, allowing your arms to swing freely in rhythm. Now, still holding your poles lightly, bend your arms slightly. Look at the angle the poles make (Figure 5.4). This is the angle you should maintain while skiing.

Diagonal poling

Now start skiing, but instead of planting your poles, keep your hands down low, maintaining the proper angle of the pole and allowing the rings to drag. The principal reason for poles is that they help in your forward thrust. They are used to the best advantage when they are set so the tip of the pole and the toe of the opposite foot are equally forward (Figure 5.5).

Concentrate on that for a minute. Take slow steps and plant the pole even with the opposite foot. Swing your right arm forward to an extended position and plant the pole as you step forward with the left foot. Swing your left arm forward to an extended position and plant the pole as you step forward with your right foot. Repeat with opposites.

Figure 5.5. The tip of the pole and toe of the opposite foot should be evenly forward.

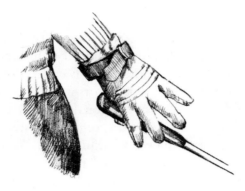

Figure 5.6. Allow your hand to go back past your hip. Your hand should be open, barely holding the pole.

Eventually the pole will help with the forward push. The pole-push/kick-glide combination will take you much farther than the strongest kick alone. It is exactly the same motion and rhythm you used when you developed your kick without poles. It is the diagonal stride—right leg-left arm working together; left leg-right arm working together. And, with the diagonal stride, a pole helps with each stride.

Keep in mind that your arm should never be straight. A straight arm is a weak arm, and you want all of the strength you can get. Also, keep the poles close to your body for added power. But on the other hand, poling itself should be done easily, without brute force. Moving by the strength of your arms alone is very tiring. Let the poles do the work. Remember, your hand will be slightly forward of the ring because of the angle of the pole, but be careful not to set the pole too far forward. That will fight your forward motion. Let your hands follow their natural course, going all the way back past your hip (Figure 5.6).

As your hand moves back, open your fingers, almost releasing your grip on the pole. Your hand should be quite open (that's why the strap is there) so you are barely holding the pole. Then, as you start to swing your arm forward, the strap will bring the pole along and you can take it up again in time for the next push.

Double poling

As you've probably suspected, there are more things to do with poles than just diagonal poling. For instance, you can use them both at the same time. This is called double poling. The technique is used to either get or maintain a faster speed than you would get with the diagonal poling. You can also use double poling when you are going on a slight downhill and don't have enough speed or momentum. You can use it when you are skiing on flat ground that is crusty. And you can use it when you get tired doing diagonal poling and want a change of pace or to take a little rest.

To double pole stand on both skis and swing both arms forward to a point even with the toes; plant the poles. Remember, the rings should be even with the toes, the hands forward of that, forming an angle. As you plant the poles, push with both arms in a quick motion with your upper body bent forward and your arms moving back past your hips in the natural way. During the poling, your body should be balanced over the skis and relaxed, knees bent forward and weight on the balls of the foot. Remember to release the grip on your poles as your arms swing back (Figure 5.7). There is no kick with this technique; the glide comes entirely from the double poling motion.

Try it again: With your weight divided on both skis, standing on the balls of the feet, knees bent, and body balanced over the skis, swing both arms forward and plant the poles opposite the toes. Push. Bend your upper body forward and allow your arms to follow through past your body. Release the grip on your poles.

Now do this exercise: After you have done a double pole, touch your hands behind your back. This is one way to tell whether you have fully extended your arms.

Figure 5.7.   Double poling motion brings both poles forward together for the push.

Double poling with a kick

This technique with the poles combines the two basic motions you have just learned. It can be used any time you are on level ground and want a change of pace. You can do it to get a good push-off on a small downhill, a good push-off on an uphill, or anytime you want to.

To do a double poling with a kick, point the left knee forward and push off with the right leg. Near the end of the kick motion, swing both arms forward and plant the double poles. Standing on both skis, enjoy the ride. As your speed begins to slow, repeat the motion. Push off with the right leg while the left knee is pointed forward; plant both poles in the double poling position and follow through. Glide (Figure 5.8).

Figure 5.8. Double Poling with a Kick combines two basic motions—Double Poling and the Kick.

Once you become familiar with this action, alternate the kicking leg as you normally would on a diagonal stride.

Now try double poling with two or more kicks. This is exactly what it sounds like from its name and can enable you to get up a good head of steam. It is a simple kick, kick, poles; kick, kick, poles. You can count it off to yourself.

There are, of course, other methods of using poles, but they are all combinations of the basic principles you have learned. Meanwhile, here are some things to remember about

Figure 5.9. If you are stabbing birds with your poles, you're holding the poles too tight. Relax.

poles: The strap should be adjusted so it is comfortable and will hold the pole in place so you can take it up easily after the release; remember to follow through completely, past your hip, then release your hold on the pole; grip the poles loosely. If you notice that your pole is stabbing birds, that's a clue you are holding on too tightly (Figure 5.9).

Robert E. Lee

6

Over hill and dale

As you have undoubtedly realized, cross-country skiing is not done entirely on a flat-as-glass area. There are hills and even mountains involved, but not, or course, to the extent you find them in Alpine skiing. If you come to a hill, you are going to climb it, if for no other reason than because it's there.

Which brings us to the next technique of Nordic skiing—going up. It's not something you will do very often, but it is something you have to know in order to get maximum fun on your skis with minimum effort. Right, minimum. Most skiers say it is easier to go up on skis than it is on foot. That's probably because when you are on skis, you go up the easiest way and expend the least amount of energy. Unless you are racing, always climb a hill slowly, relaxed. Enjoy the vista.

A method popular with several instructors is that known as "the direct approach." In this, the skier attacks the slope straight on, going up with nothing more than the regular

Figure 6.1. An uphill traverse is climbing on the diagonal across the slope. Use the regular Diagonal Stride, but shortened slightly.

diagonal stride. That's right, just straight up. As the slope steepens, it becomes necessary to shorten the stride some and, probably, push a little harder. The important thing to remember, as always, is to keep yourself loose and your knees well flexed. And be careful not to let your body lean back or forward. You should be fairly erect above the waist, hips forward, and the upper body in a slight forward lean. This helps keep your weight squarely over the skis and makes climbing easier.

When you get to the point at which you have no more glide, you can do one of two things: (a) Continue straight with a running motion, or (b) continue your diagonal stride in an uphill traverse—climbing diagonally across the hill. If you opt for the first, just pick your feet up and down as you would if you did not have skis on. It's almost a running-in-place action, except with a forward motion. In the second, just use the regular kick and glide you have been doing all along (Figure 6.1).

A good hint to remember: Keep your poles slightly

behind so they can help keep you from slipping backwards and also help push.

Side-stepping

If the hill gets so steep that you can't walk straight up or traverse any farther, switch to the next technique—side-stepping. The action is exactly what it sounds like: Side-stepping up the hill, across the grain. It is also as easy as it sounds. Turn yourself sideways, perpendicular to the hill, then just side-step up. With all of your weight on the downhill ski, lift the uphill ski up and parallel, then put it down again. Bring the downhill ski up close and parallel to it (Figure 6.2). Repeat.

You may have the feeling you are slipping down. If so, take a page from the Alpine skier's book and "hold an edge." This means the inside edge of the skis will cut into and grip the snow, thus keeping you from slipping down. The way to hold an edge is to simply turn your knees and ankles toward

Figure 6.2. Forward side-step up the hill. Lift uphill leg uphill and forward. Bring downhill ski close and parallel.

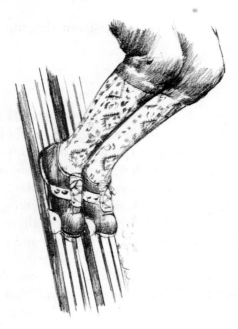

Figure 6.3. Turn knees and ankles into the side of the hill. This makes the inside, or uphill, edge of the ski grab on. It is called "holding an edge."

the hill (Figure 6.3). Voila! You're holding with the uphill ski edges. Use those edges as you go on up and you will have no problems with slipping and sliding.

There is a variation to this side-stepping action that is called "cutting down the mountain." What it is is side-stepping up and forward simultaneously. Thus, you make a ring around the mountain. Remember to take advantage of your edges and keep your poles behind for an extra boost. In "cutting down the mountain," put your weight on the downhill ski and, in the same motion, move your uphill ski about a foot and a half up the hill and about a foot forward. Shift your weight to the uphill ski and bring the downhill one alongside. Repeat, moving a pole with each step, until you are up.

Herringbone

Have you ever seen a fish skeleton intact or noticed the

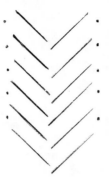

Figure 6.4.   Tracks left by herringbone technique up a hill.

Figure 6.5.   Skier herringbones up a hill by walking up with skis in a backward wedge.

pattern of woven cloth called herringbone? If you have, then you know what your tracks will look like when you go uphill using this technique (Figure 6.4). It is, appropriately enough, called herringbone, and is, in fact, V-shaped. Put your poles behind you and make your skis into a wedge—tips apart, heels together. Now, just walk up the hill in that position (Figure 6.5). Your weight should be on the whole foot, with the knees slightly turned in as you move first one ski then the other. Your poles should be slightly behind and, in this case,

Figure 6.6.   Switchbacking or tacking up a hill is climbing with a series of Zs.

your hands should be over the tops of the poles for additional support and help in going uphill. You have to hold that V with your skis or you might slip backwards. Hint: Slapping the skis down often helps give more hold.

If the hill is long and steep, making a series of Zs will make the climb easier (Figure 6.6). Hikers call this switch-backing and sailors refer to it as tacking. What it is is traversing in a forward and upward motion in one direction, then turning around and traversing in a forward and upward motion in the opposite direction. To make a 180-degree turn, assume the herringbone position, set the poles behind, and step around.

Getting down

Once you are up, like everything else, you have got to come back down, and just as in going up, there are a variety of techniques for going down. However, first you must become familiar with (a) gravity, (b) the fall line, and (c) the route.

Gravity is apparent to every skier. It dictates that skis pointed downhill will go to the bottom (tip first or tail first).

The fall line is the course they are most likely to take, straight down, Have you ever rolled a snowball or a stone from the top of a hill and watched the path it took? That path, an imaginary straight line from top to bottom, is the fall line.

The route you take down should be carefully chosen because its selection is very important. Pick a spot with a small, gentle slope and a minimum of trees and other potential hazards.

Skis parallel

Once you have your route selected, and assuming it meets the requirements of being small and gentle, the easiest way down it is straight down. Let gravity take over and follow the fall line. The position you should be in is that of the basic Alpine downhill: Set the skis comfortably parallel, shoulder-wide, about six to seven inches apart, with one ski slightly ahead of the other, and your weight divided evenly on both skis. You should be leaning slightly forward from the waist with your arms hanging loose. Bend your knees and ankles forward slightly and keep them soft and flexible, but take care not to force them forward. That force would make your heels come up and you'd be on your toes (and probably

Figure 6.7. Going straight downhill, assume a basic Alpine position: skis shoulder-wide, weight even, and a slight forward lean. Enjoy the ride and stay loose, knees bent.

your nose, too). So keep the knees and ankles bent and your heels on the skis.

Ready? Keeping the poles away from your body, lift them out of the snow and bounce, gently, in your knees. Look ahead to see where you are going. Remember, looking ahead automatically gives you better balance besides giving you the advantage of seeing what is in your path. Straighten your body, give a push, and enjoy the ride (Figure 6.7).

You have just come down the hill the "straight running-way." If you were a little wobbly, don't worry, that is a very natural thing for beginners, and that unsteadiness will gradually go away as you get a few more miles on your skis.

Go back up the hill and down again several times maintaining your weight evenly on both skis. Be sure to keep your knees and ankles bent. When you feel somewhat confident, try to gradually shift your weight, very slightly, to one ski, then back squarely on both again. Congratulations! You have just learned the first principle of turning on skis. But that is a little advanced, so file it away for now. Practice going down the slope several more times, keeping your knees bent. Try shifting your weight very slightly and coast on one ski for a while; square up and try coasting on the other.

Snowplow

Another method of going down is basically like the

Figure 6.8.   Snowplow position has the ski tips close and the tails apart in a V- or wedge-shape.

first—straight down, but with some variations. This is called the snowplow and works just like it sounds. The skis work like a snowplow in pushing the snow away, and, in turn, act like a brake with which you can control your speed or even come to a stop.

Your basic snowplow position is to have your skis set in a V or wedge with the tips fairly close together, tails apart. Square your weight over both skis and on the ball of the foot. Let your arms hang loose. Your body should have a slight forward lean (Figure 6.8). The most important single element of the snowplow is your knees. Their flexibility determines the success or failure of the snowplow. The knees control the edges, which, in turn, scrape the snow with the inside edges which, in turn, push snow out of the way. Basically, here is how it works: Going down in the knees and pushing with the heels spreads the skis and widens the snowplow; coming up in the knees brings the skis back parallel again.

Try this snowplow exercise. On level land, assume the basic position: Stand with your weight divided evenly on the balls of your feet, skis comfortably parallel about shoulder-wide, four to five inches apart. Bend your knees and force your heels out. Your skis will slide into a V shape, tips close, tails apart. Slide the skis parallel again. Repeat several times until you have the feel of sliding into a snowplow.

Now you are ready to do a snowplow in motion. At the top of a very gentle slope, assume your basic downhill position: Weight evenly divided on both skis, body with a slight forward lean, arms away from the body, skis shoulder-wide about six inches apart. Push off. As you go downhill, bend your knees and force the skis into a V position by pushing with your heels. The tips of your skis should be four to five inches apart and the tails spread proportionately. You will feel the inside edges of your skis take hold and hear a scraping sound as they cut into the snow. Do you find yourself slowing down? Good. Before you come to a stop and while you still have momentum, relax your knees and come up; your skis will automatically come back parallel again and you will, once more, be in the straight running-way down.

Combination

On a longer slope, go back and forth from straight to snowplow to straight to snowplow as many times as you want to. This will automatically change your speed each time. If you look back at your tracks, they will look like a long series of almost eights (Figure 6.9).

As you can see, the snowplow is an excellent way to maintain good control over your speed. It is simply a matter of learning to control and handle your edges, and the best way to become proficient at that is to put many miles on your skis. Hint: Concentrate on keeping your weight square on both skis and take care not to turn your knees in too much (on either one ski or both) because that all too often results in crossed skis which, in turn, results in a belly flop (Figure 6.10).

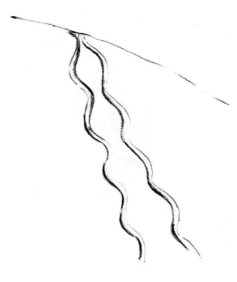

Figure 6.9. (Above and right) Going downhill in a series of snowplow/straight motions will leave a track that resembles loose figure eights.

Figure 6.10. (Below) Crossed skis often result in a belly flop.

Figure 6.11. Traverse position for downhill is the same as the straight-running position, except the downhill ski is slightly ahead.

Traverse

In going up the hill we learned a technique called the traverse—moving sideways across the face of the slope. That is also a good way of going down the hill. In the traverse, you would assume your basic straight running position with one variation: Stand on both skis with slightly more weight on the downhill ski. Otherwise, arms away from the body, body with a slight forward lean, knees bent, and skis set parallel shoulder-wide about six inches apart, with the uphill ski slightly ahead (Figure 6.11). Push off and cut the steepness of the slope by moving at an angle across it. If you are moving too fast, slow down with the snowplow: With bent knees, force your skis into a V position with the tips four to five inches apart and the tails spread proportionately. When you are at a comfortable speed and feel well in control, come up in the knees again and let the skis come back parallel.

Side-step

There are two other methods of going downhill. If the slope is very steep and offers no area gentle enough to

Figure 6.12. Side-step down a hill the same way you go up, except in reverse.

accommodate your level of skiing, you can side-step down in the same manner you side-stepped up, except in reverse. In other words, with poles out to the side and weight on the uphill ski, lift the downhill ski and set it down several inches below. Transfer your weight and bring the uphill ski down and parallel (Figure 6.12). Repeat until you are at the bottom. The important thing to remember is to use your edges. Keep your knees and ankles pointed into the hill. This automatically puts you on the hillside or gripping edge of your skis.

Walk

If the slope is simply too steep to chance even side-

Figure 6.13.   If the hill is too steep, take off your skis and walk down.

stepping, take off your skis and walk down (Figure 6.13). It is absolutely the safest and sanest thing to do. Don't be embarrassed to do it. You know the old adage: Better safe than sorry. You better believe it. Don't take a chance. It's not worth it. Unless you do something stupid like schussing a mountainside that is far and away above your skiing ability, you aren't going to get hurt on cross-country skis. So do the sensible thing.

You can also go downhill à la Alpine which, for the purpose of cross-country skiing, involves a few elementary turns. These will be discussed in the next chapter.

Falls

Now, no matter how sensible and careful you are, you are going to take a fall or two. So it is important that you know how to fall. If you are going too fast, your balance is gone, and you are totally out of control, you know you are going to fall. So before you do, just sit down. Falling is a very natural thing for all skiers and is nothing to be embarrassed about. Simply sitting down is the easiest and safest way to fall (Figure 6.14).

Figure 6.14. If you think you are going to fall, just sit down.

Another way to fall is to stretch out to the side and let yourself down. It is important that you get a slide with your body fully extended (Figure 6.15). You are going to say, "Oh yeah, sure," when you hear this, but: Do try to relax when you fall. And avoid tucking yourself into a ball (Figure 6.16). That will likely send you rolling head over skis. So stay loose and relaxed and either just sit down or, with body fully

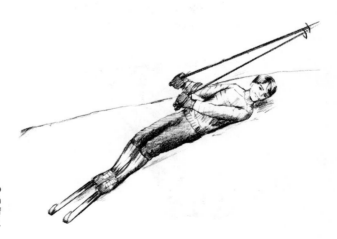

Figure 6.15. Another way to safely fall is to lean and stretch out sideways and let yourself down easily. Keep poles away.

Figure 6.16. Avoid tucking yourself into a ball.

extended, stretch over to the side and plunk yourself into something soft.

Getting up

After the fall, there is always the necessity of getting back up on your skis again. The first thing to do is plan what you are going to do. In other words, get organized. First, take the pole straps off your wrists. Second, untangle your skis, if necessary. Sometimes the best way to do that is to roll over on your back with the skis in the air overhead (Figure 6.17), then put them back together on the snow. If you are on the flat, put your skis parallel again, pointing in the same direction. Because your heel is free, you get into a genuflect position as you go to your knees. Then, holding one pole on either side for balance and support, stand up (Figure 6.18).

Figure 6.17. Sometimes the easiest way to untangle skis is to roll over on your back and get the skis in the air.

Figure 6.18. With poles on
either side, raise to your knees
in a genuflect position.

If you are on a slope, set your skis down parallel to each other and downhill from you (Figure 6.19), set straight across the face of the hill. Be sure they are neither facing uphill nor downhill. Taking care not to let your ankles get ahead, bend your knees. Holding both poles together for maximum strength and support, push yourself up by placing one hand near the baskets or rings and the other farther up the pole (Figure 6.20).

Another way to get up is to sit on the tails of your skis, bend your knees, reach forward between your legs, and take hold of either your ski boot or the binding. Then just pull yourself up (Figure 6.21). Or you can set your skis in a snowplow position (a V or wedge with the tips fairly close together and the tails spread). Plant one pole on either side of you, not behind or in front. Then just lift yourself into an upright position (Figure 6.22).

And, of course, if all else fails, take your skis off, stand up and put the skis back on again.

Figure 6.19.   Roll your skis downhill of you but not pointing downhill. Hold your poles on the uphill side.

Figure 6.20.   Push yourself up using both poles for added strength and support.

Figure 6.21.   Lean forward and grab your boots or bindings and pull yourself up.

Figure 6.22.   With skis in a
snowplow position, set poles to
the side and lift yourself.

Canadian Government Office of Tourism

7

Making turns

You can go just about anywhere on cross-country skis with what you have learned already; however, you will have more fun if you add a few basic Alpine turns to your repertoire. So here goes:

Step turn

You have already made the first turn—the step turn you did back in the beginning. You stood on one ski, lifted the other and set it down several inches to the side, and brought the other ski to it (Figure 7.1). That was your first change of direction. Repeat until you have gone 180 degrees and are facing the opposite direction. You don't need your poles for this, and it is easier to simply hold them in your hands and carry them. But if you want them, particularly for balance, whatever you do, don't drag the poles, lift them out of the snow and set them down again.

Figure 7.1.   The Step Turn is the first turn you learned. Try that turn again now.

Kick turn

Another way to change directions while standing still is known as the kick turn. I'll warn you, the first time you try this you are going to feel somewhat akin to a contortionist, but it's really not all that tough. It just seems that way, so I suggest the first time you try it, do so without skis in the privacy of your bedroom. And, if you can do it in front of a full-length mirror, all the better.

Begin with the skis parallel and the weight on the right

Figure 7.2.   The first time you try a Kick Turn, do it without skis. It's not as difficult as it looks.

ski. Turn your body so it faces to the left and put both poles behind you on either side of your body. Pick up your left ski and swing it around a complete half-circle so it is facing the opposite direction; set it down. There you are standing with both poles behind you and with your left ski facing left and your right ski facing right. Stay that way until you regain your balance. Shift your weight to the left ski and, using your left pole for balance, swing your right ski around so it is parallel to the left; set it down. That's it, you are facing in the opposite direction (Figure 7.2).

Feel pretty smug, don't you. Well, now the trick is to go the other way. Need help? With your weight on your left ski, pick up the right one and swing it around so it faces in the opposite direction. Regain your balance. Pick up the left ski and set it down parallel to the right. See, it really is pretty easy.

The kick turn is very useful and can be executed almost anywhere you are standing still, including halfway up, or halfway down, a mountainside. Now for some moving turns.

Ski around the corner

Look around and pick out a spot where you want to

Figure 7.3. Ski Around the Corner is done just like walking around a corner.

turn. Ski to it using your regular kick and glide rhythm. When you reach the spot, instead of stoping, pick up a ski and turn it toward the direction in which you want to go. Bring the other foot parallel.

Don't try to make something difficult out of this. It is just like walking around a corner: While moving, pick up your right ski and put it down in the direction you want to turn. Bring the left ski parallel as you are continuing your touring stride (Figure 7.3). Repeat if necessary until you are around the corner. Be sure to keep your knees bent.

Skate turn

This turn got its name from a turn done in ice skating. Doing it on the flat is a particularly good way to learn about your edges and how to control them. The turn itself is made

Figure 7.4.   Skate Turn is the same motion an ice skater employs.

by using the inside edge of the ski to push off, then gliding while the skis are brought parallel again.

To do the skate turn, do several touring strides, then glide on both skis with your weight squarely on them. Keep your knees bent. Go into a slight crouch and push in the direction you want to go. If you are going to the right, pick up the right ski while the left leg pushes off. Then transfer the body weight to the right ski (Figure 7.4). Repeat until you have completed the turn. Does this feel familiar? It should. It is a basic exercise you did back at the beginning when you were moving around the figure eight pattern.

A variation of the skate turn is to do it along with a double poling motion. For example, if you are turning to the left, begin by standing on both skis with your weight divided evenly. Swing both arms forward, reaching with your poles; set the poles down and push with them. Glide on both skis with your weight square. Go into a slight crouch position and point the left ski to the left. Using the inside edge of your right ski, push off. Bring the right ski parallel to the left and stand on both skis. Repeat.

Snowplow turn

So much for turning on the flat, let's go downhill. This is the easiest downhill turn to make. From its name, you have probably already figured out what it is, and you already know the principle of the turn. You will recall that in learning the basic snowplow, you transferred your weight very slightly to one ski and turned in the opposite direction. Now you are going to make turns for real.

Start by assuming the basic snowplow position: Weight on the balls of the feet, square on both skis, knees flexed, body with a slight forward lean, knees and ankles slightly forward, arms loose at your sides, and skis comfortably parallel about shoulder-wide. Bend your knees and force your heels out so the skis form a V with the tips about four or five inches apart and the tails spread proportionately. Push

Figure 7.5.   A Snowplow Turn
is made from the wedge
position with a shift in weight.

off and, holding a snowplow position, very slowly transfer your weight slightly to the right ski. If you are doing it correctly, you should be turning to the left (Figure 7.5). Concentrate on the right ski and don't worry about the left, it will follow right along.

Try it this way: At the beginning of your descent, push your right heel slightly more than the left, then stay square over both skis. Push a little more with the right heel and transfer a little more weight to the right ski. Come back square over the skis again, and slowly shift your weight to the left ski. See, it does work in both directions.

You make a turn by shifting your weight to the side opposite the direction in which you want to go. In other words, if you want to turn to the left, transfer your weight to the right ski. And, it is very important that you keep some weight on both heels. An unweighted ski is a lost ski. Also, keep both skis in the snowplow position all of the time: Do *not* try to push one ski ahead of the other.

If you think you are doing everything properly, but are still not making a turn, it is probably because you are edging too much. Your knees may be turned in too much, causing you to ride on the edges instead of the flat bottoms. Start with a very narrow snowplow, with heels fairly close together. A narrow wedge makes the edges a little flatter. It is better not to try making too many turns at first. Rather, make a small turn, a little change of direction, before trying to make a severe turn. Learn to lean more, shift your weight and relax.

Stem turn

This turn is a more advanced turn and is one, like the snowplow, that is also used by Alpine skiers. The snowplow is the basis for the stem turn, so have the former well in mind. Begin by assuming the basic straight running position: Slightly more weight on the downhill ski, skis set parallel shoulder-wide, arms to the side, and body with a slight forward lean. Traverse across a gentle slope to the left. To make a right turn, shift your weight to the right ski and push with your left heel so the left ski slides into a wedge pointed in the direction in which you will turn. It should look like a half-snowplow. Now transfer your weight to the left ski and let the body lean very slightly over the left ski as the ski turns into the new direction. When the turn is completed, the right ski should slide parallel to the left and form a new traverse (Figure 7.6).

Try the stem turn in the opposite direction: To turn left, shift your weight to the left ski and push with your right heel so the right ski slides into a wedge pointed in the direction of the turn. Transfer your weight to the right ski and let the body lean very slightly over the right ski as the ski turns into the new direction. The turn is complete, and the left ski should be parallel to the right, forming a new traverse.

After you have done several of these stem turns in both directions, instead of sliding the turning ski into position, pick it up and try to plant it in the direction of your turn. Later on, you will probably find you don't need to open your turning ski nearly as much and, thus, you will be able to make faster turns.

Figure 7.6. A Stem Turn involves going into a half-snowplow position as you go around the corner.

Telemark

Back in the beginning, you were introduced to a knee-bending exercise that many skiers do almost daily as a warm-up. You slid one ski forward and almost touched the opposite knee to the ski. Try the same thing again now: Standing on both skis with your weight evenly divided, slide your left ski forward about 18 inches until the left instep is approximately even with the right ski tip. Bend your knees into a genuflect position; the left one should be right over the front ski and the right heel should be well off the ski. Sink down and almost touch your right knee to the ski. Take care to keep your back straight. Bend your knees, not your back. Hold it, don't move. You have just assumed the basic Telemark position (Figure 7.7).

The Telemark is the oldest and most traditional of all skiing movements, both Alpine and Nordic. It was the original way to make a turn and is still used today, although mostly for fun and for exhibition. The basic position is also a

Figure 7.7. To assume the basic Telemark position, slide one ski forward and bend your knees into a genuflect pose.

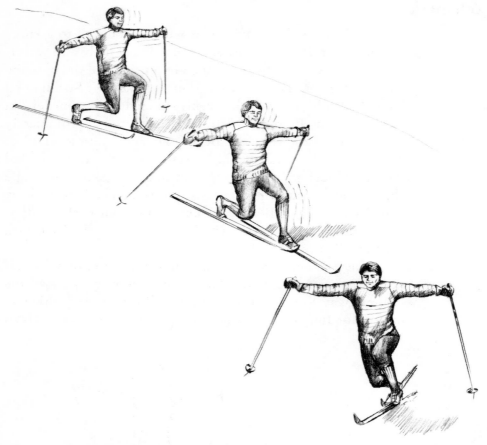

Figure 7.8.   The Telemark position is one way to make a turn—the oldest method of making a turn in all of skiing.

good way to regain your balance, as well as a way to add stability.

Practice going into the Telemark position, first with the left ski forward, then with the right. When you are comfortable doing it, practice going into position from a straight running glide. Find a little hill and start down in the basic free running position. As you are moving down the hill, slide into the Telemark position—first with the left ski forward, straighten up, then right ski forward, and straighten up again. You will probably find your poles very helpful in maintaining your balance the first few times you try this exercise, so take advantage of them. That's one of the reasons you are toting them along.

Feel ready to try a turn? Put your arms out to the side for balance and start out in a slight traverse. Assume the Telemark position and turn the left ski tip in the direction of your right turn. Keep your weight evenly divided on both skis. That's it. Unless you didn't maintain your balance, you made a turn to the right (Figure 7.8). Try it again, but to the left.

Remember, when doing the Telemark (and all of the other turns, for that matter) don't force it. Take your time and let each turn come naturally. You are in no hurry. Make long, sweeping turns. Relax. You have control, you can stop, and you can turn. Suddenly, you know what skiing is all about. It's a great sport. Enjoy it.

Robert E. Lee

8

Putting it all together—rules of the snow

Now that you know the basics of cross-country skiing and have practiced to the point where you feel comfortable and reasonably confident, it is time to take a tour. But before you do, there are some things you should know.

The first rule of cross-country skiing is: Never ski alone unless you are on a golf course or in a park with many other people in the immediate area.

Snow

Snow of course is an important factor in skiing. You already know that if you have three or four inches on top of a grassy or otherwise soft base, you have plenty of snow and don't have to worry about hurting the bottoms of your skis. If you come to a paved or gravel road with either no snow or not enough to glide across, the safest thing to do is take your skis off and carry them across.

There are different kinds of snow, and each has its effect

Figure 8.1. Beginner skiers often experience a "hot foot." It comes from trying to hold on with the toes.

on your skiing. If the snow is cold and powdery, you aren't likely to get much of a glide. Where there is any significant amount of snow depth, unless you are skiing in a prepared or well-used track, chances are you will sink into the snow and, generally, find the going harder.

In warm or soft snow, you will find the going much easier, and you will look terrific! Soft snow is easier to ski on and is especially good for your balance. You will find yourself going faster and farther, too.

Hotfoot

The first several times out on cross-country skis, you may experience a strange sensation—a hot foot. The bottoms of your feet feel as if they are burning up. It's a common experience for novices of both Nordic and Alpine skiing and comes from trying to grab with your toes. Truly. The first time your skis feel a little wobbly, you are probably going to do the natural thing—try to hang on by curling your toes. Result: Hot feet (Figure 8.1). You can avoid that by concentrating on keeping your toes relaxed. Consciously stretch them out flat and keep them relaxed. It won't be long before skiing comes easier and the curled toes will go away, taking the burning right along with them.

Planning

No one can over emphasize the importance of advance planning. A good rule to follow is: Don't go touring without thorough planning.

Your first tour should be relatively short, so pick out an area where, at no point along the route you are more than a half-mile from a major road or an occupied lodge or home. If the area is in a national forest or a park, check with the ranger for suggested areas in which to tour, areas to be avoided, and pick up maps if available.

When you are in a group, remember you can travel only as fast as the slowest person. Take the weakest person into consideration when planning a tour; don't overdo and remember no matter how far you go, you have to come back.

Change leaders

Regardless of the snow conditions, when you are in a group going through virgin snow, it is a good idea to change leaders frequently to avoid one person's becoming overtired. The easiest way to do this is for the leader to go 50 or so yards, then step off to the side and fall in at the end, while the next person takes the lead (Figure 8.2).

Take it slow, unhurried, your first few times out. It is very easy to become overenthused and thus, overdo. You will find yourself tired with still miles to go. For beginners, a rule of thumb is approximately a mile per hour, including stops to catch one's breath, stops to take in the scenery, and stops to figure why one is off stride.

Figure 8.2.   When you're touring in a group, take turns breaking trail.

Lunch

So if you are going to be gone a few hours, it is always nice to take along a light lunch, or at least a snack. Lunches can be fun to pack and can challenge your imagination. Keep in mind, though, that you will probably be carrying it on your back, so try to pack light. Also, select things that keep well in the cold and are eaten chilled, unless you want to pack along a Thermos. A European-style lunch that is always popular is a bottle of wine, hard salami, aged cheese that is well-wrapped to protect it from freezing and a loaf of French bread. Very tasty.

The European-style lunch is fine for short tours because you don't have to tote it far. If you are going a longer distance, then choose something easier to carry than a wine bottle. Pick lighter weight foods that are high in protein and, therefore, good sources of energy. Remember that cross-country skiing is one of the highest calorie-burners there is, so you want to replace that energy you have used.

Dried fruits, such as raisins, figs, and apricots, are excellent sources of high energy and are easy to carry. Cheeses are another good source of protein: the more aged, the more protein it offers. In general, bypass the processed or soft cheese and select a cheddar or the drier cheeses available (I stop just short of Parmesan).

You can have a super snack by making your own protein snack bars: Thin and sweeten peanut butter with honey to taste; form balls or "logs"; roll in granola and wrap individually.

Fruit Leather is another take-me-along that is not only rich in energy, but is easy to make, easier to handle, and so light in weight you hardly know it's there. So to deviate from cross-country skiing to cooking, here is how to make Fruit Leather:

Select any fruit, either fresh or canned—the yellow ones, such as peaches and apricots, are particularly good. If canned, drain very well. Puree in a blender until the fruit is absolutely smooth. Use an approximate ratio, depending upon your sweet tooth, of one cup puree to one tablespoon honey or sugar. Line a big sheet pan or jelly-roll pan with plastic wrap (waxed paper, even if oiled, sticks) and spread sweetened pureed fruit very, very thin. Bake at the lowest temperature possible—150 degrees F.—four hours or until done in the oven. The leather is done if it won't stick when touched. Remove from oven and pan, peel off plastic, and roll up in another sheet of plastic wrap. Once Fruit Leather is dry, it can be stored in a cupboard. Good stuff.

Additional equipment

Besides food, there are some things you should automatically carry whenever you are touring out in the country. One of the most essential is sunglasses. Even though the sun is lower in the sky during winter, the glare off the snow can be highly detrimental to the eyes. Sunglasses offer the necessary protection.

A light windbreaker is another good thing to carry, as are an extra pair of wool socks, mittens, hat, a wool sweater, or down parka. An emergency kit should also be in the pack.

If you are a large group touring together, designate one person as leader, then outfit that person with a pack that includes a knife, screwdriver, pliers, steel wool (for fixing worn-out screw holes), extra parts (such as screws, wires, cables, and thong for touring bindings), extra sweater, windbreaker, cap, gloves, sunburn lotion, cork and scraper, paraffin, water, first aid kit, and sunglasses.

Emergency kit

The more touring you do, the more touring you will want to do, and the farther afield you are going to be traveling. It is well to adopt the Boy Scout motto and "Be Prepared." Make yourself an emergency kit that includes the basics for warmth, strength, and safety. The kit should be small enough that you won't be tempted to leave it home for the sake of room in your backpack, yet it should fulfill the purpose. Your emergency kit should include:

Metal can, one-pint size, with a tight sealing lid, for cooking
Candle, for light and for starting fire
Matches
Salt, for helping overcome fatigue
High-protein foods, for energy
Bouillon cubes for food, energy, and warmth
Tea bags for making a hot drink
Space blanket for signaling and for heat
Sealing tape for emergency patching

Other things you might want to take along are maps, a compass, flashlight, an extra ski tip, aspirin, and fruit.

Figure 8.3.   Do not try to stop yourself by jamming the poles in front of you. This is very dangerous to the skier and the poles.

Words of caution

Before going anywhere on cross-country skis, you should carefully check your equipment to make sure it is in good condition. And make a checklist so you won't forget anything.

It is very important that you look at the weather and be alert for warnings of a storm that might be moving in your direction. If you see such indications, turn around immediately and go home. No matter how well prepared, you are no match for Mother Nature, and she can be very unforgiving. So take the advice of the experts, and play it safe. It is better to cut a tour short today and ski again tomorrow. Or next week.

Another word of caution. If you are going downhill and think you are going too fast do *not* jam your poles in front of you in an attempt to catch yourself (Figure 8.3). No matter how sensible this action may seem, it is one of the most dangerous things you can do. A pole slamming into the stomach can do irreparable damage.

After the first two or three lessons, my Nordic friend suggested that I come back after I had put a hundred miles on my skis. As usual, that was good, sound advice, and that's the same advice I'm passing along to you now. You know the basics, what to do, and how to do it, so what you need now is more and more practice.

Racing

It was suggested to me one of the better ways to get that practice: Enter citizen class cross-country ski races. Me, race? Ridiculous! But the encouragement continued above my objections and I'm glad. Racing proved to be one of the most fun and most rewarding things I have ever done.

To be sure, I didn't win the first race I entered. In fact, I was well back in the pack. I had fallen, slipped, and generally tried so hard that I fought the natural rhythm and motion of cross-country skiing. I also learned an important lesson of racing that day: When someone behind you yells "track," it means move over and let him or her pass. Nevertheless, I did finish the race with a determination and a pledge to do better next time.

Just as had been promised, because I had practiced and skied and learned better control of my skis and myself, I did do better in the next race; and the subsequent races were that much better again.

So don't be afraid to give racing a try. Most communities and resorts where cross-country skiing is even mildly popular have citizen races. The beauty of them is that, generally, there are classes for everyone: Juniors, high school and college age boys and girls, beginner men, beginner women, intermediate, advanced, and expert of both sexes. So you compete against your own sex in your own age group and your own level of ability. And, more important, generally the distances of the race courses increase with ability, so beginners and children usually go a much shorter route than the experts.

Whether you decide to participate in or just watch citizen cross-country races, at least get out and use your skis. Enjoy them and reap the benefits they offer—being out-of-doors in Mother Nature's own special winter playground, exercising and burning up calories, and increasing your general physical fitness. The direct result is a good night's sleep.

Conclusion

Cross-country skiing is a great participation sport, and I am grateful to my mentor for having gotten me off the right way. I'm glad you are learning that, too.

Happy skiing!

Glossary

Basket—metal ring attached near the base of a ski pole to keep the pole from sinking too deep in the snow. Often called *ring*.

Boots—the key to good skiing and the single most important piece of equipment. Not the place to save money.

Camber—a bow in the skis under the foot area that allows the ski bottoms to touch and lift off the snow when the skier's weight shifts.

Diagonal stride—the basic cross-country motion with the right leg/left arm and the left leg/right arm moving forward and back together.

Fall line—imaginary line from top to bottom of a hill, running the path of least resistance—straight down. If a snowball were dropped at the top of a hill and allowed to roll down, its chosen path would follow the fall line.

Frozen gorilla—(1) a person so tense and unrelaxed that his movements resemble King Kong of the Arctic; (2) a person so wrapped up in cold weather gear that he cannot move.

Gaiters—water-repellent cloth that covers the boot top, instep, ankle, and at least the lower leg, and keeps the snow out. A good investment.

Gripper—found on the bottom of Nordic skis and makes the skis adhere momentarily to the snow, enabling the skier to push forward. The gripper can be wax, strips of fur, fish-scale pattern, a step-pattern or replaceable strips.

Herringbone—a method of climbing a hill. Skier puts skis in a backwards wedge and walks up holding that position.

Holding an edge—turning the knees and ankles in to the hill, which makes the uphill edge of the skis grab on and hold. Holding an edge keeps the skier from slipping sideways down a slope.

Kick—a force attained by pushing off with the ball of one foot to propel yourself forward.

Kick turn—a change of direction made standing still. Midway through the turn, the feet face in opposite directions.

Mousetraps—the clamp-style bindings favored by Nordic skiers. Also called *pin* or *pole-operated bindings*.

Nordic norm fit—the one-size-fits-all concept of matching boot soles with bindings.

Paraffin—a good item to carry along to keep the bottoms of nonwax and both tops and bottoms of all skis free of ice.

Pin bindings—the clamp-style, step-in bindings favored by Nordic skiers. Also called *mousetrap* or *pole-operated bindings*.

Pole-operated bindings—clamp-style, step-in bindings favored by Nordic skiers. Also called *mousetrap* or *pin bindings*.

Poles—held in the hands and used in rhythm to push uphill, speed across the flat, slow the downhill speed, and help lift fallen skiers out of the snow. Also frequently used by beginners to help maintain balance. Sometimes called a *crutch*.

Ring—metal ring attached near the base of a ski pole to keep the pole from sinking too deep into the snow. Also called *basket*.

Side-step—method of moving sideways, either on the flat or up and down a hill. The motion is to move one foot 12 to 16 inches, then bring the other close to and parallel.

Snowplow—a position that has the skis in a V or wedge for either going downhill or turning. The result is, as the name implies, like a snowplow in that the snow is pushed aside out of the path.

Stem (turn)—an intermediate level change of direction in which the skier opens the skis into a half-snowplow position as he goes around the corner.

Switchbacking—way of traversing up or down a hill using a series of Zs. Also known as *tacking*.

Tacking—method of going up or down a hill, traversing across the face in a series of Zs. Also known as *switchbacking*.

Telemark—one of the original ski positions. Now used to regain one's balance or for exhibition turns.

Traverse—moving crosswise, diagonally across the face of a slope.

Wax—a crystalline substance applied to the bottoms of wax skis that grips and releases snow as the skier shifts weight from ski to ski. Also known as *gripper*.

Index